SAMMY BAUGH, LARRY BROWN, JOHN RIGGINS, BOBBY MITCHELL, CHARLEY TAYLOR, JERRY SMITH, JIM LACHEY, CHRIS SAMUELS, RUSS GRIMM, JOE JACOBY, LEN HAUSS, DEXTER MANLEY, CHARLES MANN, DAVE BUTZ, DIRON TALBERT, CHRIS HANBURGER, KEN HARVEY, SAM HUFF, DARRELL GREEN, PAT FISCHER, KEN HOUSTON, MARK

THE STORY OF THE WASHINGTON REDSKINS

MURPHY, MARK

MOSELEY, SAMMY BAUGH, LARRY BROWN, JOHN RIGGINS, BOBBY MITCHELL, CHARLEY TAYLOR, JERRY S

JIM

LACHEY, CHRIS SAMUELS, RU

JOE JACOBY, LEN HAUSS, DEXTER MANLEY

86

THE STORY OF THE WASHINGTON REDSKINS

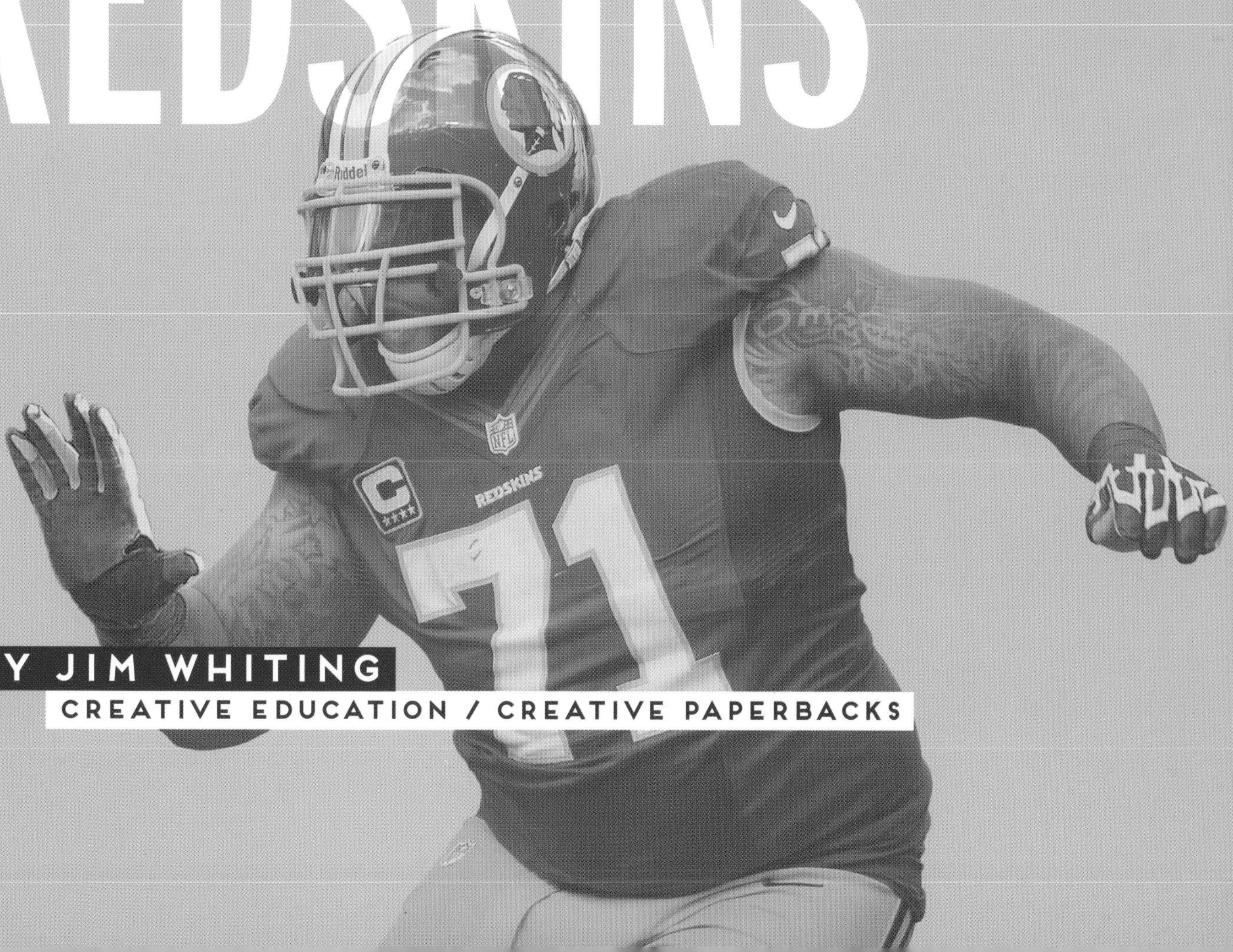

BY JIM WHITING

CREATIVE EDUCATION / CREATIVE PAPERBACKS

PUBLISHED BY CREATIVE EDUCATION AND CREATIVE PAPERBACKS
P.O. BOX 227, MANKATO, MINNESOTA 56002
CREATIVE EDUCATION AND CREATIVE PAPERBACKS ARE IMPRINTS OF THE CREATIVE COMPANY
WWW.THECREATIVECOMPANY.US

DESIGN AND PRODUCTION BY BLUE DESIGN (WWW.BLUEDES.COM)
ART DIRECTION BY RITA MARSHALL
PRINTED IN CHINA

PHOTOGRAPHS BY AP IMAGES (ASSOCIATED PRESS), GETTY IMAGES (ROBERT BECK/SI, BRUCE BENNETT STUDIOS, ROB CARR, NATE FINE/NFL, JAMES FLORES/NFL, FOCUS ON SPORT, JED JACOBSOHN, G. NEWMAN LOWRANCE, JOHN MCDONNELL/THE WASHINGTON POST, BOB PETERSON/TIME & LIFE PICTURES, PRO FOOTBALL HALL OF FAME/NFL, PAUL SPINELLI, RICK STEWART, SHAWN THEW/AFP, ROB TRINGALI/SPORTSCHROME, HARRY WALKER/MCT), NEWSCOM (ROY K. MILLER/ICON SPORTSWIRE DGE, SHANE ROPER/CAL SPORT MEDIA, ARNIE SACHS/CONSOLIDATED NEWS PHOTOS)

NAMES: WHITING, JIM, AUTHOR.
TITLE: THE STORY OF THE WASHINGTON REDSKINS / JIM WHITING.
SERIES: NFL TODAY.
INCLUDES INDEX.
SUMMARY: THIS HIGH-INTEREST HISTORY OF THE NATIONAL FOOTBALL LEAGUE'S WASHINGTON REDSKINS HIGHLIGHTS MEMORABLE GAMES, SUMMARIZES SEASONAL TRIUMPHS AND DEFEATS, AND FEATURES STANDOUT PLAYERS SUCH AS JOHN RIGGINS.
IDENTIFIERS: LCCN 2018061073 / ISBN 978-1-64026-161-7 (HARDCOVER) / ISBN 978-1-62832-724-3 (PBK) / ISBN 978-1-64000-279-1 (EBOOK)
SUBJECTS: LCSH: WASHINGTON REDSKINS (FOOTBALL TEAM)—HISTORY—JUVENILE LITERATURE.
CLASSIFICATION: LCC GV956.W3 W44 2019 / DDC 796.332/6409753—DC23

FIRST EDITION HC 9 8 7 6 5 4 3 2 1
FIRST EDITION PBK 9 8 7 6 5 4 3 2 1

COVER: TRENT WILLIAMS
PAGE 2: JORDAN REED
PAGES 6–7: CLINTON PORTIS

74

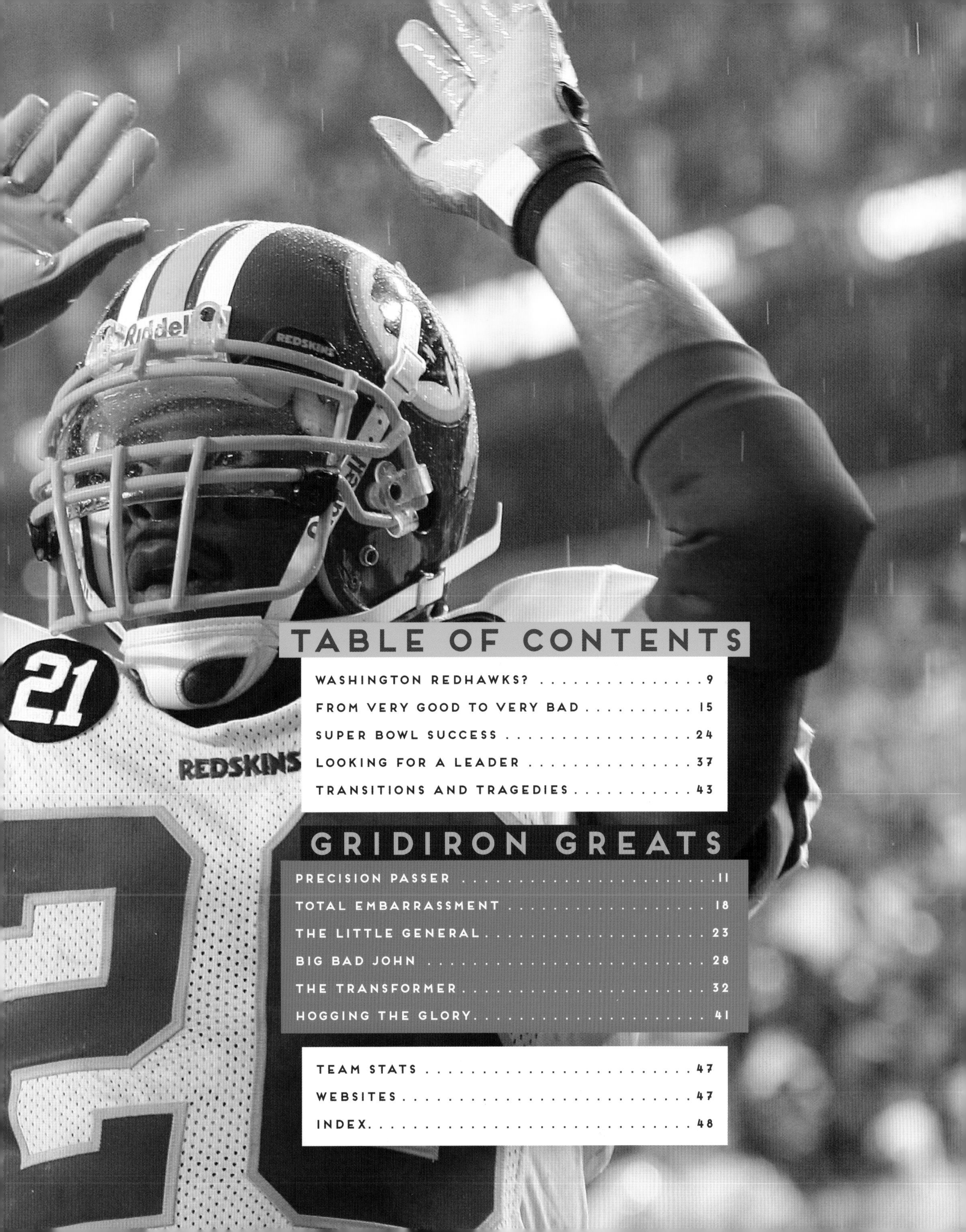

TABLE OF CONTENTS

GRIDIRON GREATS

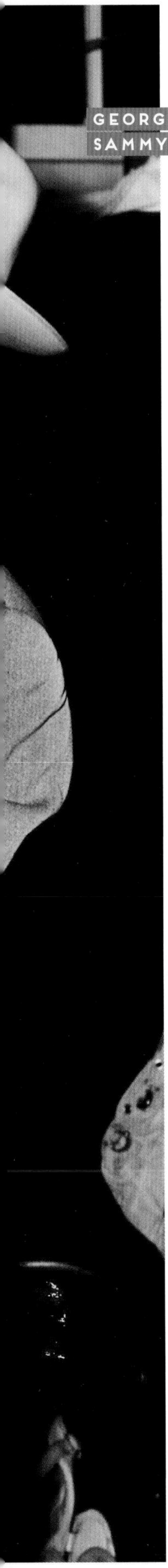

GEORGE MARSHALL AND QUARTERBACK SAMMY BAUGH

WASHINGTON REDHAWKS?

In the early 1930s, professional football was a relatively minor sport. Several teams played their games in Major League Baseball parks. Often, they took the same name as the baseball team. They felt it gave them more legitimacy. In 1932, businessman George Marshall founded a National Football League (NFL) team in Boston. The team played in the same stadium as the Boston Braves. So he named it the Boston Braves.

The team finished just 4–4–2. Marshall wanted his team to improve. He decided that it would play "Indian football." It had the reputation for being wide-open and exciting. It was especially known for lots of passing and trick plays. The NFL had even had an all-American Indian team, the

Oorang Indians. They played in 1922 and 1923. Marshall hired one of the most famous American Indian coaches, William "Lone Star" Dietz. Dietz claimed that he was part Sioux. He often stalked up and down the sideline wearing a Sioux headdress.

Before the 1933 season began, Marshall moved the team. He made an agreement with the Boston Red Sox to play at Fenway Park. He had to change the team name. But he was committed to keeping the American Indian theme.

However, what to call the team soon became the hurdle. It had to be a name in common usage. That meant he couldn't use any of the names of local tribes. Hardly anyone outside the Boston area would have heard of them. In addition, most were too hard to pronounce. Marshall couldn't use "Indians," either. Several short-lived Cleveland teams had taken that name.

Marshall narrowed his choices down to three: Warriors, Chiefs, and Redskins. He chose Redskins. There were probably several reasons. Marshall may have thought it would help make his team stand out more. Hardly any other teams in the country had that name. Also, in 1929, a film called *Redskin* was praised for its sensitive portrayal of an American Indian athlete. Marshall was a friend of the star. In addition, Redskins sounded somewhat similar to Red Sox. And in that era, Redskins didn't have the negative associations it does now.

Several American Indian players joined the team. Marshall photographed them wearing traditional native dress. The team jerseys had an Indian head symbol on the

WASHINGTON REDSKINS BAND MEMBER

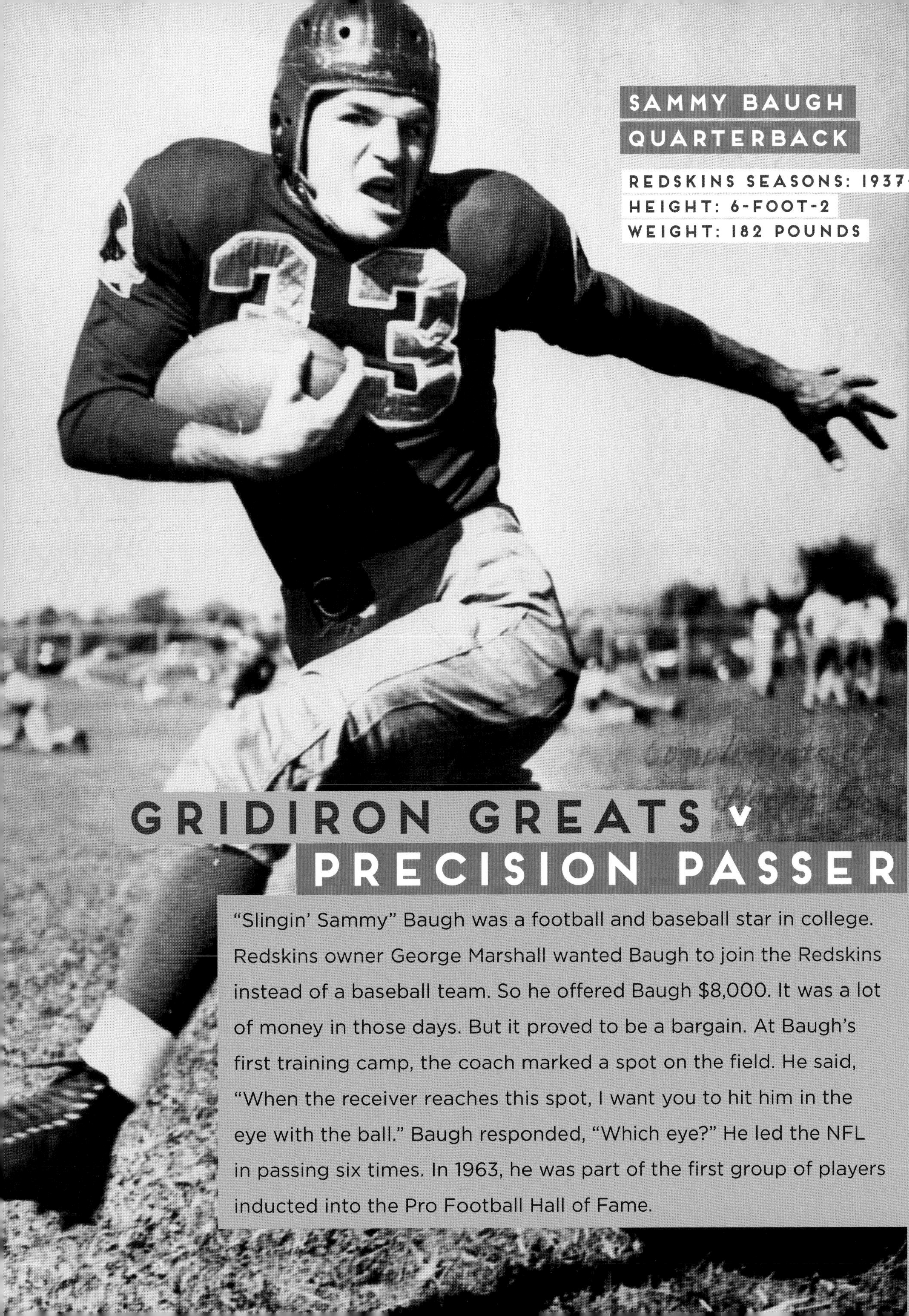

SAMMY BAUGH
QUARTERBACK

REDSKINS SEASONS: 1937–52
HEIGHT: 6-FOOT-2
WEIGHT: 182 POUNDS

GRIDIRON GREATS
PRECISION PASSER

"Slingin' Sammy" Baugh was a football and baseball star in college. Redskins owner George Marshall wanted Baugh to join the Redskins instead of a baseball team. So he offered Baugh $8,000. It was a lot of money in those days. But it proved to be a bargain. At Baugh's first training camp, the coach marked a spot on the field. He said, "When the receiver reaches this spot, I want you to hit him in the eye with the ball." Baugh responded, "Which eye?" He led the NFL in passing six times. In 1963, he was part of the first group of players inducted into the Pro Football Hall of Fame.

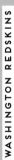

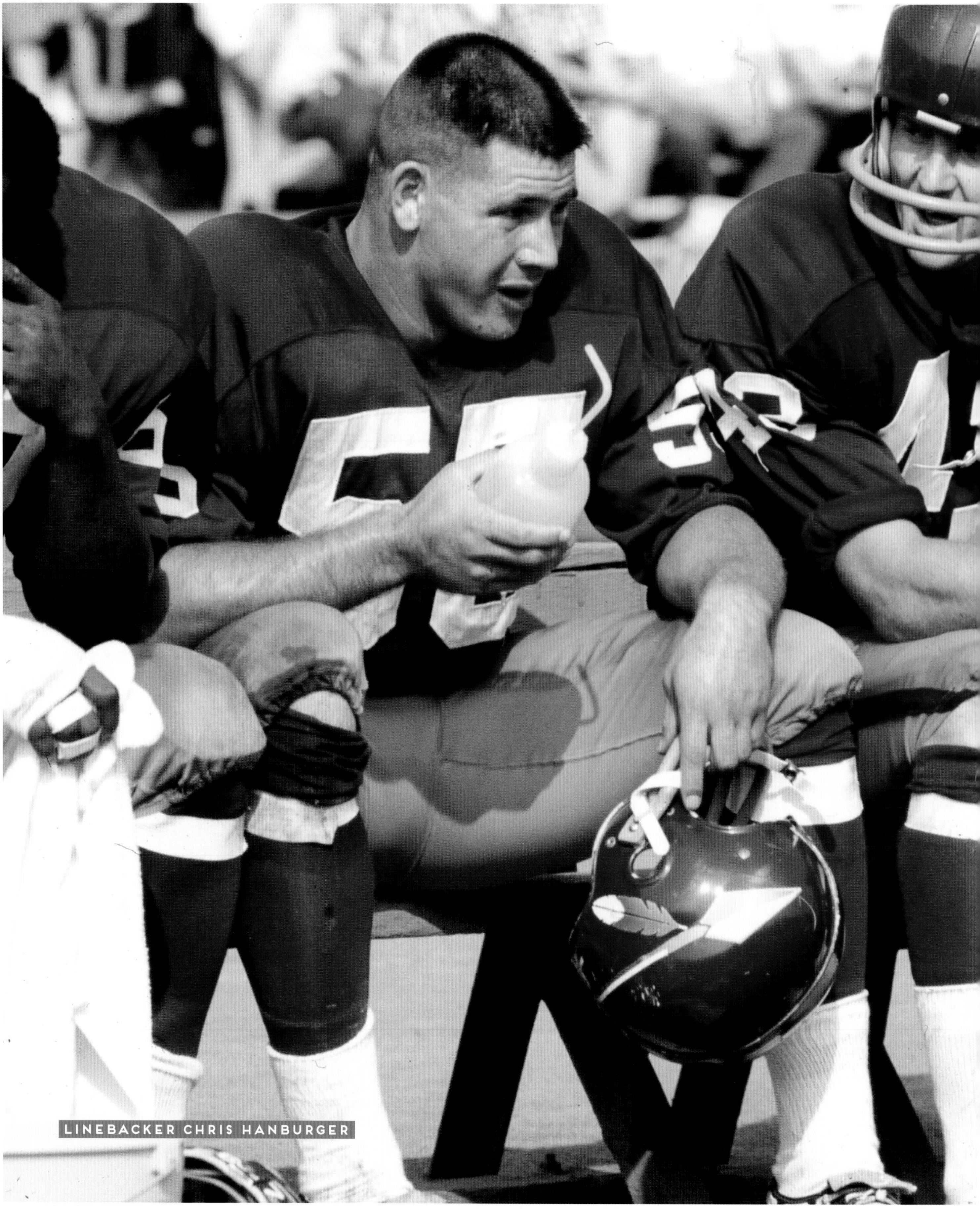

LINEBACKER CHRIS HANBURGER

"THE NAME OF THE TEAM IS THE WASHINGTON REDSKINS AND WILL REMAIN THAT."

—2017 TEAM STATEMENT

front. All the players put on war paint for the first game of the 1933 season.

But by the 1970s, many people objected to the name. They said it was insulting and racist. They asked the team to change it. The team refused. Recently, pressure to change the name has increased. In late 2017, there was an announcement: The team had decided to change its name to Redhawks. Part of the announcement showed a new logo. It featured a hawk in the team's traditional burgundy and gold colors.

The claim was not real. But as one of the members of the group that had produced this bit of fake news explained, "This is an issue that comes up very dramatically.... We wanted to make it immediate and urgent by allowing people to imagine a world where that mascot is gone, the name is changed, and see how people react to it."

In response, the team issued a statement: "The name of the team is the Washington Redskins and will remain that for the future." Owner Dan Snyder added that the name is a "badge of honor." It seems likely that the controversy will continue in the upcoming years.

1942 WASHINGTON REDSKINS

FROM VERY GOOD TO VERY BAD

The new name and playing field did not improve the team's record. In 1933 and 1934, it remained at .500. Dietz left. The Redskins plunged to 2–8–1. They rebounded in 1936. They finished at 7–5. It was their first winning season. They played the Green Bay Packers for the NFL championship. They lost, 21–6.

By then, Marshall was unhappy in Boston. The team did not draw many fans. He blamed the Boston media. He said they paid more attention to a field hockey game than to the team's participation in the NFL title game. Marshall moved the team to his hometown of Washington, D.C., the nation's capital. Attendance was no longer an issue. There the team

SAMMY BAUGH

was based farther south than any other NFL team at the time. It became the "home team" for millions of football fans in the South.

In 1937, the Redskins featured a new star. He was rookie quarterback Sammy Baugh. He earned the nickname "Slingin' Sammy" in college. In his first year in the NFL, Baugh led the league in passing. At the time, passing was a far less prominent part of the professional game than it is now. Baugh had 81 pass completions in 11 games. He averaged 102.5 passing yards per game. The Redskins traveled to Chicago for the NFL Championship Game. They faced the powerful Bears. The field conditions were awful. Baugh said that it "froze solid with jagged clods sticking up. I've never seen so many people get cut up in a football game." Still, Baugh played well. He threw three touchdown passes. The Redskins won, 28–21. It was their first NFL title.

TACKLE TURK EDWARDS

In 1940, Washington again faced Chicago in the NFL Championship Game. This time, though, the Bears walloped the Redskins, 73–0. Despite that humiliating loss, the Redskins stayed strong. They earned their second league title by defeating the Bears in the 1942 championship game, 14–6. In 1943, they met the Bears in the championship for the fourth time in seven years. The Bears won, 41–21.

Two years later, the Redskins met the Cleveland Rams in the championship game. At that time, the goalposts were located at the front edge of the end zone. Early in the game, Baugh passed from his end zone. The ball hit the goalposts. It bounced backward and out of the end zone. The play was ruled a safety. The Rams received two points. Those

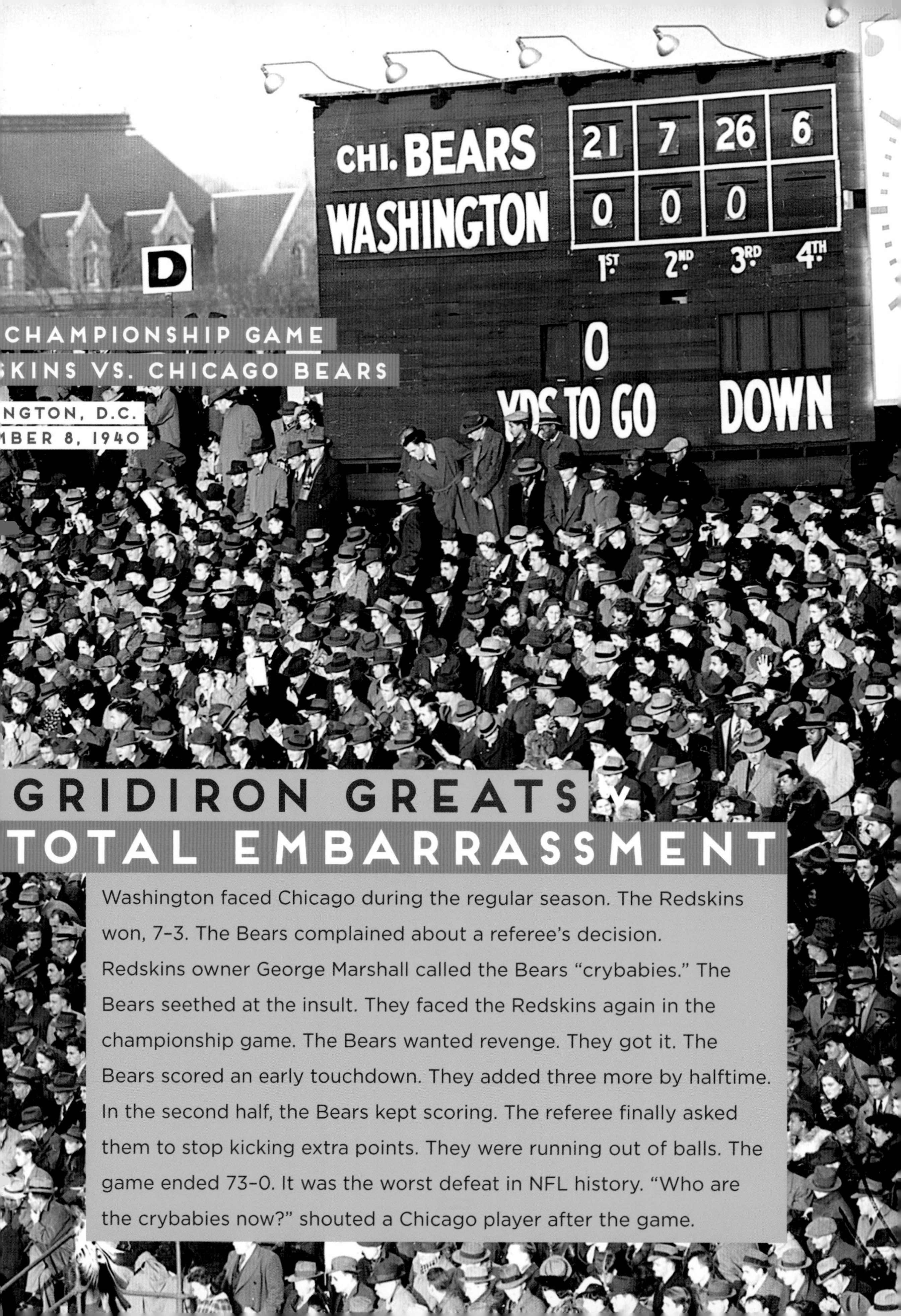

CHAMPIONSHIP GAME
KINS VS. CHICAGO BEARS

NGTON, D.C.
1BER 8, 1940

GRIDIRON GREATS
TOTAL EMBARRASSMENT

Washington faced Chicago during the regular season. The Redskins won, 7–3. The Bears complained about a referee's decision. Redskins owner George Marshall called the Bears "crybabies." The Bears seethed at the insult. They faced the Redskins again in the championship game. The Bears wanted revenge. They got it. The Bears scored an early touchdown. They added three more by halftime. In the second half, the Bears kept scoring. The referee finally asked them to stop kicking extra points. They were running out of balls. The game ended 73–0. It was the worst defeat in NFL history. "Who are the crybabies now?" shouted a Chicago player after the game.

9

9 TURNOVERS ALLOWED

519

519 TOTAL YARDS AGAINST

"[THE FIELD] FROZE SOLID WITH JAGGED CLODS STICKING UP. I'VE NEVER SEEN SO MANY PEOPLE GET CUT UP IN A FOOTBALL GAME."

—SAMMY BAUGH

two points made all the difference. The Rams won, 15–14. "There was dirty work at the cross-bars here [in Cleveland] yesterday as the Rams won their first National Football League championship in history," joked the *Pittsburgh Press*. "Instead of maintaining their usual strict neutrality, those cross-bars showed a definite prejudice for the home team."

Slingin' Sammy retired in 1952. He had set almost all the NFL's passing records. His number 33 jersey is the only one officially retired by the Redskins. By then, the team had entered a dark period. From 1946 to 1968, Washington had just three winning seasons. Twice it won just one game. Still, fans cheered the efforts of standout players. One was small quarterback Eddie LeBaron. The "Little General" thrilled fans with his scrambling ability. He could pass around and over much bigger defenders.

COACH VINCE LOMBARDI

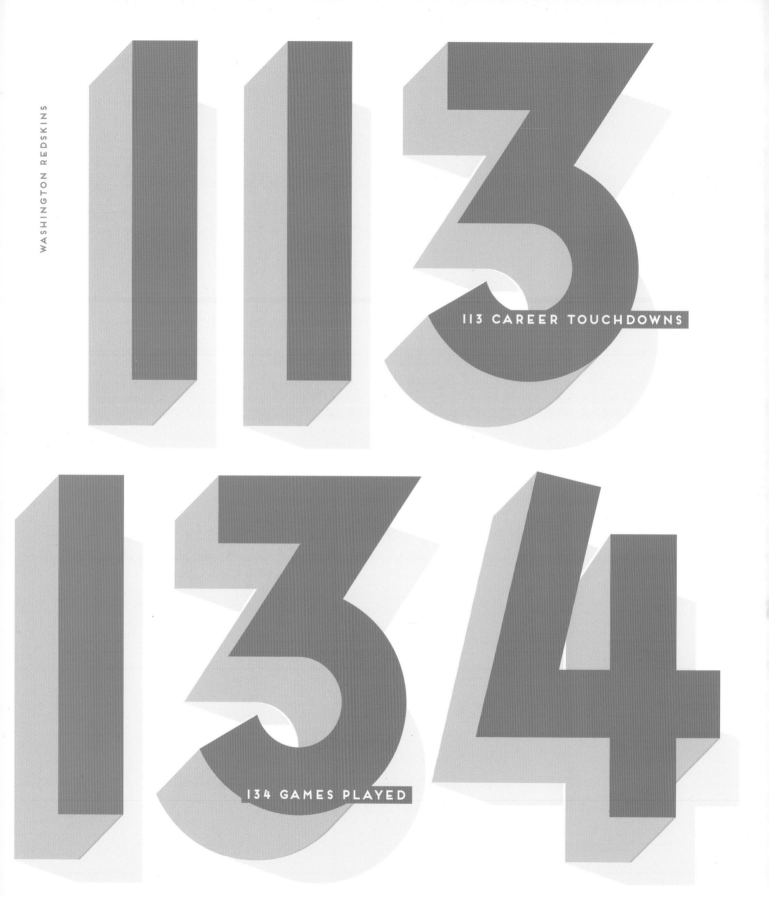

113

113 CAREER TOUCHDOWNS

134

134 GAMES PLAYED

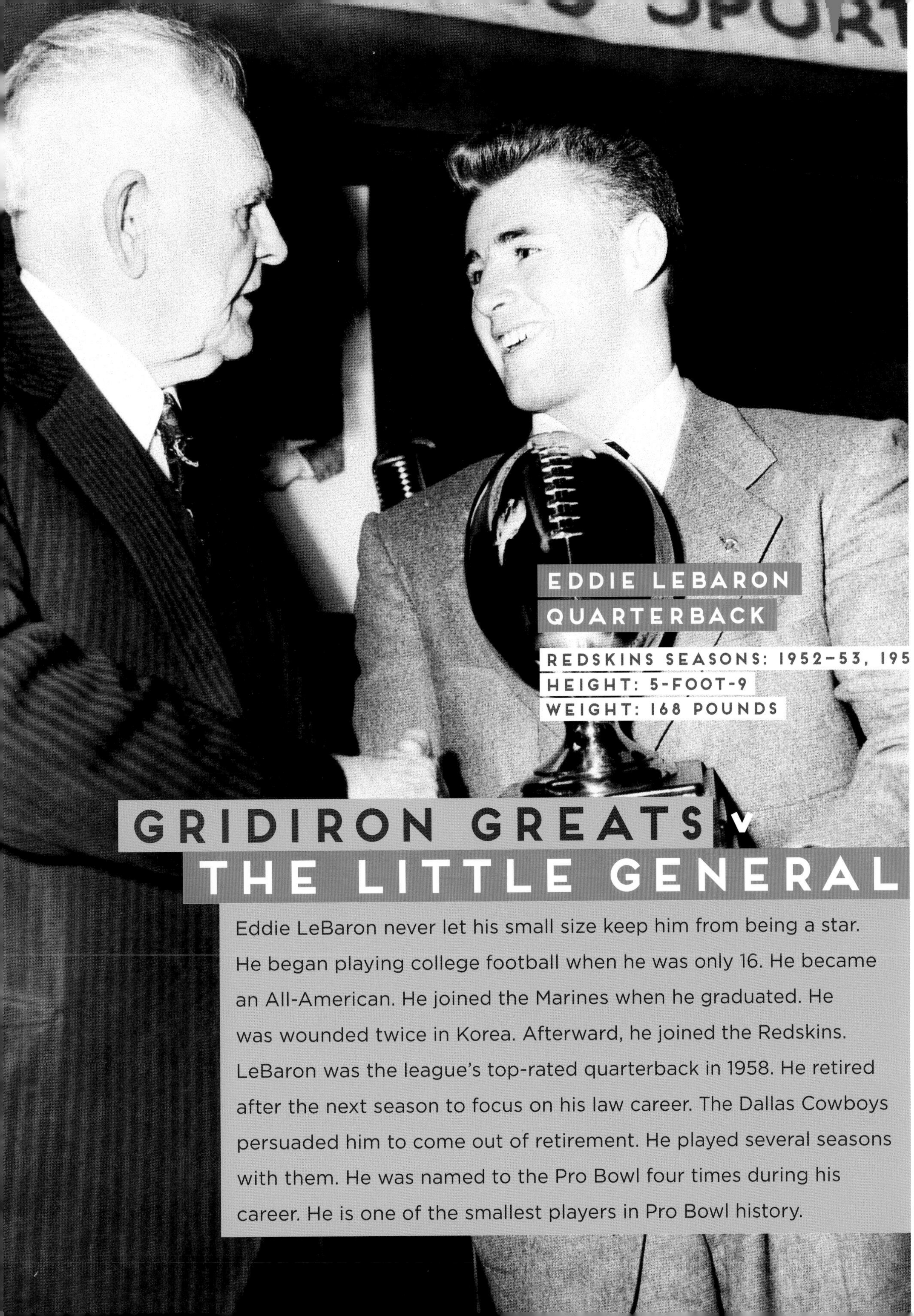

EDDIE LEBARON
QUARTERBACK

REDSKINS SEASONS: 1952–53, 1955–59
HEIGHT: 5-FOOT-9
WEIGHT: 168 POUNDS

GRIDIRON GREATS
THE LITTLE GENERAL

Eddie LeBaron never let his small size keep him from being a star. He began playing college football when he was only 16. He became an All-American. He joined the Marines when he graduated. He was wounded twice in Korea. Afterward, he joined the Redskins. LeBaron was the league's top-rated quarterback in 1958. He retired after the next season to focus on his law career. The Dallas Cowboys persuaded him to come out of retirement. He played several seasons with them. He was named to the Pro Bowl four times during his career. He is one of the smallest players in Pro Bowl history.

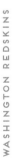

SUPER BOWL SUCCESS

QUARTERBACK SONNY JURGENSEN

Washington finally became a winner again in 1969. Hall of Fame coach Vince Lombardi came out of retirement to lead the team. Lombardi reminded his players that he had never coached a losing club. "And nothing is going to change that," he insisted. He was right. Washington finished at 7–5–2. Sadly, during the off-season, Lombardi died from cancer. The Redskins reverted to their losing ways in 1970.

In 1971, George Allen took the reins. He did not want to develop young

9

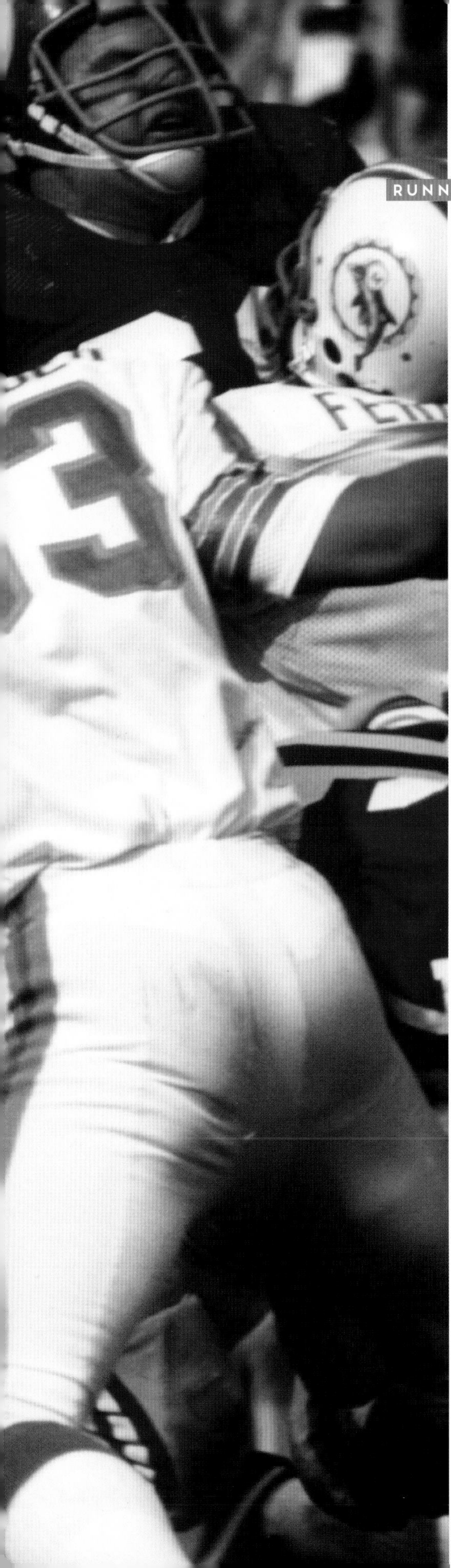

RUNNING BACK LARRY BROWN

talent. Instead, he traded future draft choices for established stars. Fans and writers soon began calling the Redskins the "Over the Hill Gang." Allen's gamble paid off. The team made the playoffs for the first time in 26 years. The next year, the Redskins earned their first trip to the Super Bowl. The undefeated Miami Dolphins beat them, 14–7.

The Redskins made the playoffs three more times from 1973 to 1976. But they failed to reach the Super Bowl again. In 1978, Allen was replaced. The Redskins remained an average team. Joe Gibbs took over as coach in 1981. His offense was led by quarterback Joe Theismann and burly running back John Riggins. Teammates called Riggins "The Diesel." He roared through the line like a powerful truck. Gibbs added several huge blockers to the offensive line. They were known as "The Hogs."

In the 1982 season, Gibbs led the Redskins to the Super Bowl. It was exactly 10 years after their first Super Bowl

GRIDIRON GREATS

BIG BAD JOHN

John Riggins had one of the most famous plays in team history. It was a 43-yard touchdown run that gave the Redskins the lead in Super Bowl XVII. Riggins possessed an unusual combination of power, speed, and cockiness. He once came to training camp sporting a Mohawk haircut. Another time, he showed up wearing only shorts and a derby hat with a feather. Riggins had a contract dispute with the team before the 1980 season. So, he left. He returned one year later. "I'm bored, I'm broke, and I'm back," he told fans. He still holds team career records for rushing attempts, rushing yards, and rushing touchdowns.

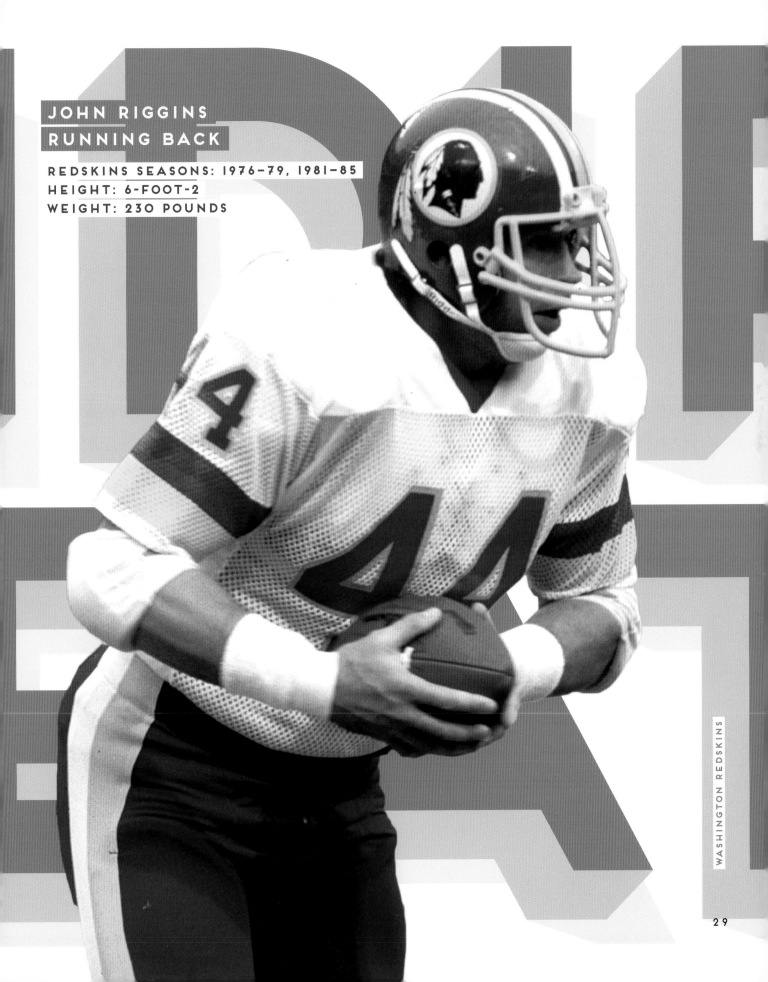

JOHN RIGGINS
RUNNING BACK

REDSKINS SEASONS: 1976–79, 1981–85
HEIGHT: 6-FOOT-2
WEIGHT: 230 POUNDS

JOE THEISMANN

appearance. Early in the fourth quarter, Miami led, 17–13. Washington faced a fourth-and-one on the Dolphins 43-yard line. Everyone expected Riggins to simply dive forward for the first down. Instead, The Diesel slid to his left. He broke through the tightly packed defenders. Then he raced for a touchdown. Washington added one more score. The Redskins won, 27–17. It was their first Super Bowl triumph.

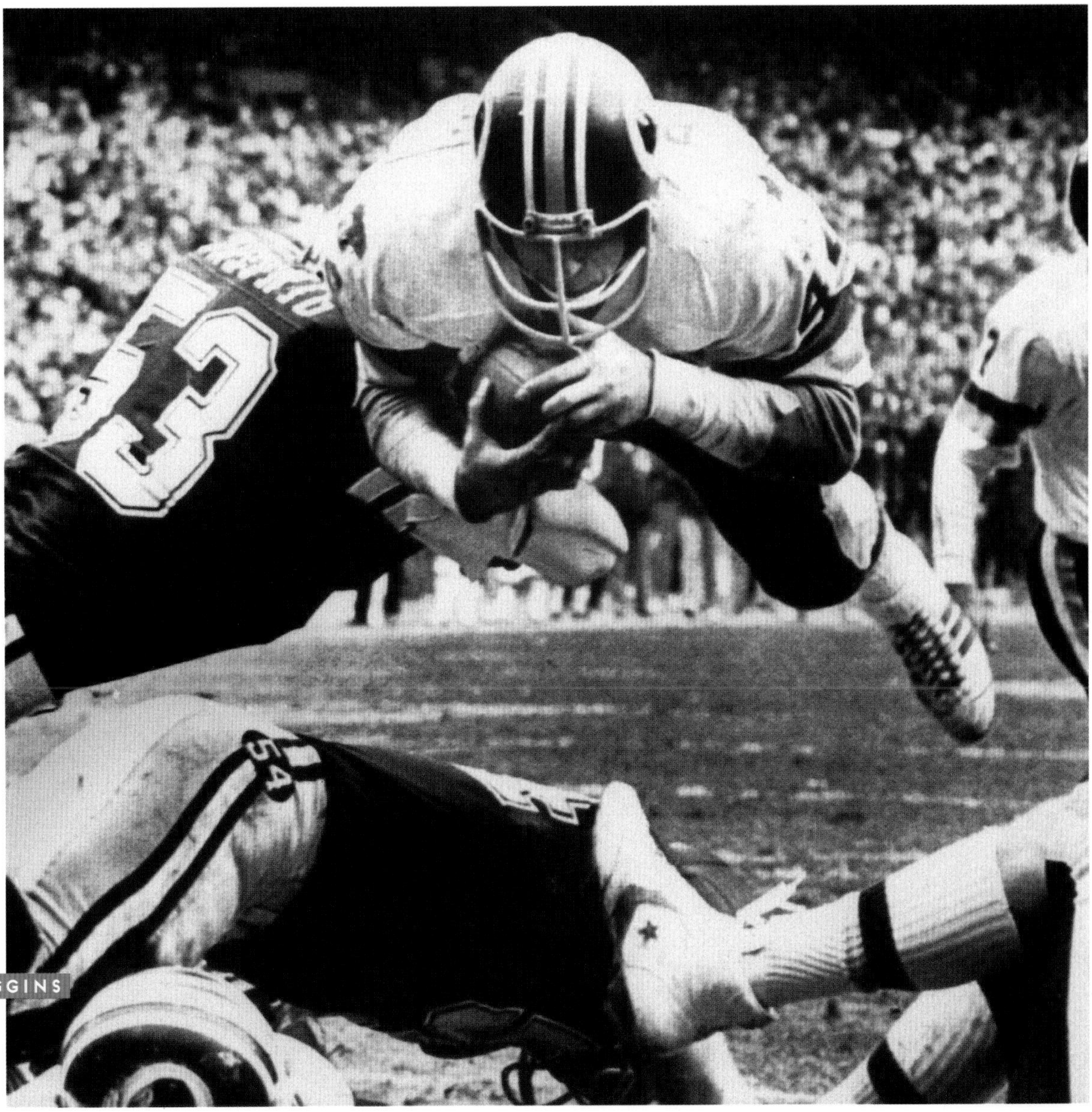

JOHN RIGGINS

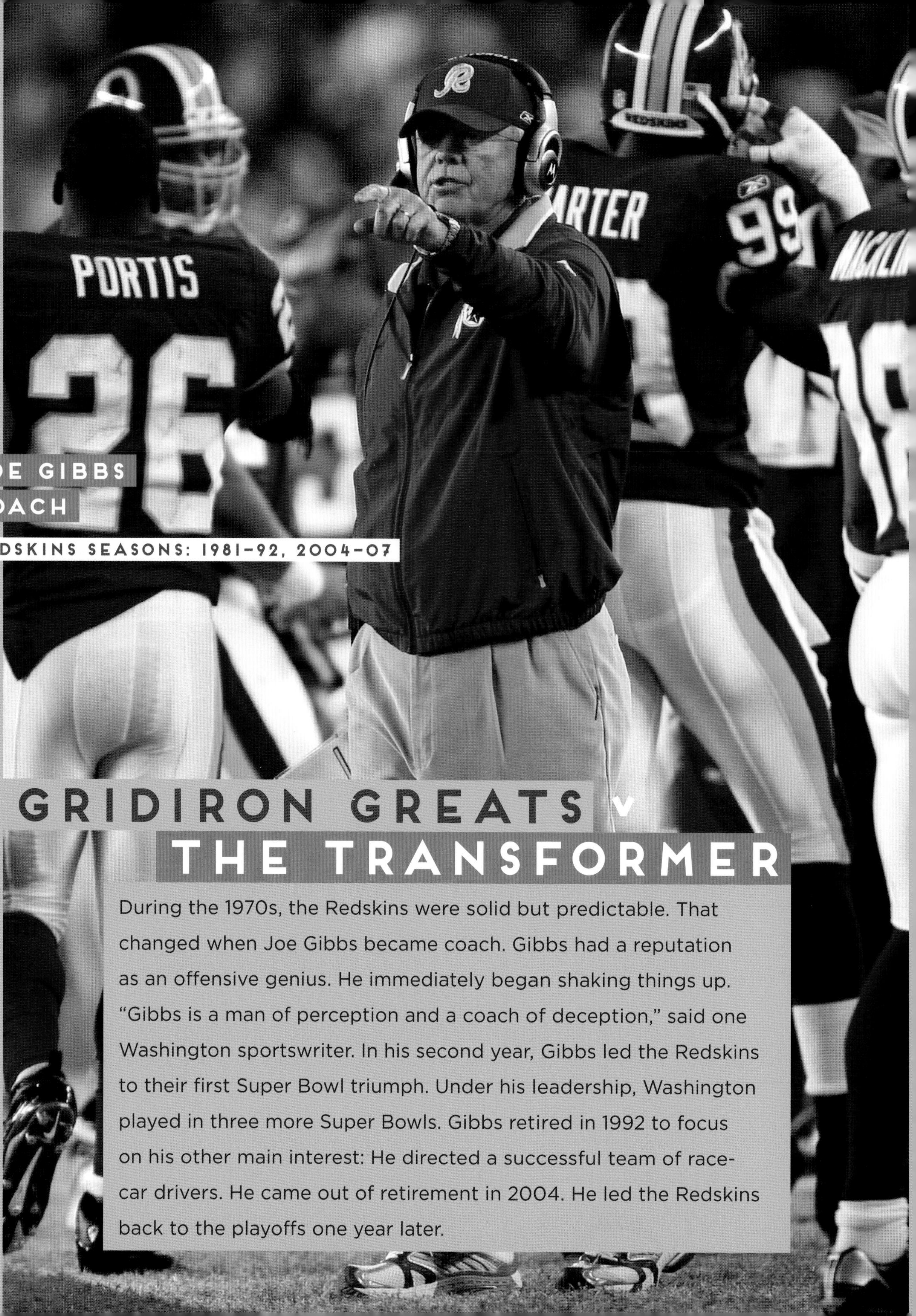

JOE GIBBS
COACH

REDSKINS SEASONS: 1981–92, 2004–07

GRIDIRON GREATS
THE TRANSFORMER

During the 1970s, the Redskins were solid but predictable. That changed when Joe Gibbs became coach. Gibbs had a reputation as an offensive genius. He immediately began shaking things up. “Gibbs is a man of perception and a coach of deception,” said one Washington sportswriter. In his second year, Gibbs led the Redskins to their first Super Bowl triumph. Under his leadership, Washington played in three more Super Bowls. Gibbs retired in 1992 to focus on his other main interest: He directed a successful team of race-car drivers. He came out of retirement in 2004. He led the Redskins back to the playoffs one year later.

154

154 CAREER WINS

248

248 GAMES COACHED

DOUG WILLIAMS

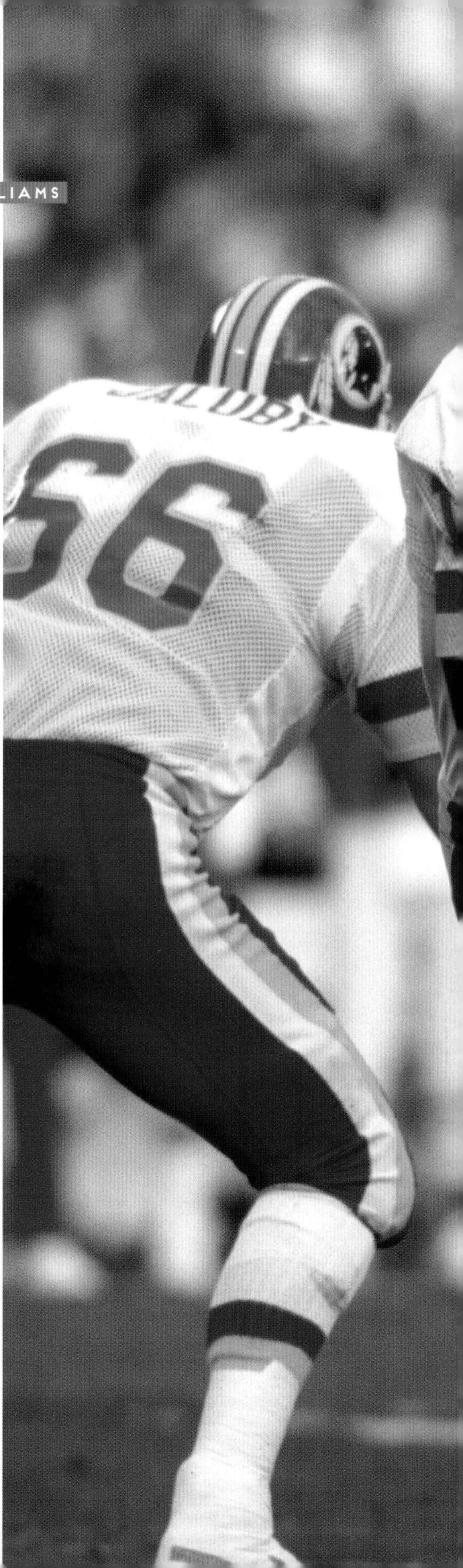

Washington was even stronger the next year. The team set several league scoring records. The Redskins finished 14–2. But they fell to the Los Angeles Raiders, 38–9 in the Super Bowl. "We were the best team in the history of Washington football," said Theismann. "But that will never be known because we didn't win a Super Bowl."

In 1987, quarterback Doug Williams led Washington to another Super Bowl. The Redskins faced the Denver Broncos. The Broncos galloped ahead, 10–0. Then Williams let his strong right arm take over. He tossed four touchdown passes in the second quarter. The Redskins went on to win, 42–10. Williams suffered a back injury the next season. Mark Rypien replaced him. Just a few years later, Rypien guided the Redskins to Super Bowl XXVI. They defeated the Buffalo Bills, 37–24.

RUNNING BACK CLINTON PORTIS

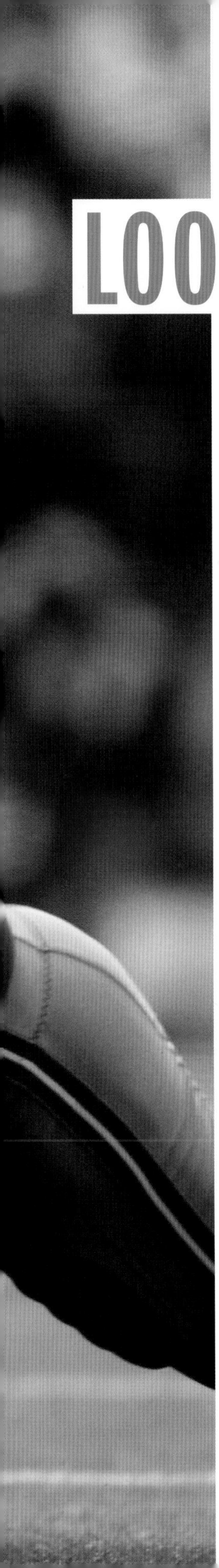

LOOKING FOR A LEADER

Gibbs retired in 1992. Under his leadership, the Redskins had appeared in four Super Bowls. They won three of them. They did not reach the playoffs again until 1999. Then, the Tampa Bay Buccaneers knocked them out in the divisional round. "We had a bunch of guys who played well together and were tight like a family," said linebacker Eddie Mason.

Soon, the excitement of 1999 faded. The team spent millions of dollars to add veteran stars. But the Redskins hit a slump. The team played "musical

LEFT: RUNNING BACK STEPHEN DAVIS

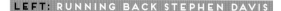

coaches" between 2000 and 2003. It had four (including two in one season). The team had especially high hopes for Steve Spurrier, who took over in 2002. He had won the 1996 college national championship with the Florida Gators. "We're going to turn FedExField into the loudest stadium in the country," he said. Unfortunately, much of the noise consisted of boos. Spurrier's teams suffered through losing two losing seasons. He resigned.

Joe Gibbs returned in 2004. He told reporters that he purposely did not wear the Super Bowl rings he had earned in his earlier stint with the Redskins. "We're focused on the future," he said. "I love the challenge of doing something that's almost undoable." Facing his new challenge head-on, Gibbs made significant changes. He traded for running back Clinton Portis. His straight-ahead running style reminded fans of Riggins. Gibbs also signed veteran quarterback Mark Brunell. But Washington finished just 6–10.

The Redskins rebounded in 2005. They finished with 10 wins. They roared into the playoffs. They beat the Buccaneers, 17–10. But they lost to the Seattle Seahawks in the next round. "We hit a rough point this year when we were 5–6, and guys could have pointed fingers," said Portis. "But nobody did. We've got more to look forward to next year."

Unfortunately, "next year" did not go as fans hoped. Portis was injured. Brunell played inconsistently. Halfway through the season, Gibbs replaced him with second-year quarterback Jason Campbell. Although Campbell posted respectable numbers, the change-up did not help. The season ended in a disappointing 5–11 record.

DEFENSIVE BACK DARRELL GREEN

"THE HOGS" OFFENSIVE LINE

GRIDIRON GREATS
HOGGING THE GLORY

In the 1980s, the Redskins boasted one of the most famous offensive lines of all time. The players who made up the line were called "The Hogs." Offensive coordinator Joe Bugel gave them their nickname. "A Hog," Bugel explained, "is a guy who gets down and does a dirty job without wanting to be beautiful." Many fans showed up at games wearing hog noses, hog hats, and hog T-shirts to show their love for their hardworking heroes. The Hogs also included one non-lineman. That was running back John Riggins. "He has the personality of a Hog," said tackle George Starke.

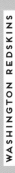

36

SEAN TAYLOR

TRANSITIONS AND TRAGEDIES

Fans braced themselves for another poor season in 2007. They were pleasantly surprised. Washington won five of its first eight games. Portis was healthy. Campbell improved throughout the season. By midseason, the Redskins appeared to be on their way to the playoffs. Then they lost three tight contests in a row.

Tragedy struck in late November. Burglars invaded the home of All-Pro safety Sean Taylor. One of them shot Taylor. He died soon afterward. Gibbs tried to console his players. “Sometimes in life, maybe some of the best things happen to you after you have been kind of crushed,” he said. The team made a heroic comeback. It won its last four games. It went to the playoffs. But it fell to the Seahawks in the first round.

Two days later, the 67-year-old Gibbs surprised his players and Washington fans. He announced that he would once again be retiring as head coach. He wanted to spend more time with his family. Under new coach Jim Zorn, Washington began the 2008 season by winning four of its first five games. But it could not keep up the momentum. Its 8–8 record was not good enough for the playoffs. Washington slumped in 2009. The Redskins finished at 4–12. Zorn was fired.

Washington hired former Denver coach Mike Shanahan. He had taken the Broncos to two Super Bowl championships. But there were no postseason trips for the Redskins in either 2010 or 2011. The team tried to improve its chances for the 2012 season. The Redskins drafted Robert Griffin III with the second overall pick in the NFL Draft. The quarterback became known as "RGIII." He turned out to be everything the team wanted. He had the highest rookie quarterback rating in NFL history. He led the Redskins to a 10–6 mark. They made their first playoff appearance in five years. Unfortunately, RGIII suffered a leg injury at the end of the season. Washington lost in the first round of the playoffs.

RGIII was never the same. Washington limped through the next two years. Kirk Cousins replaced Griffin in 2015. He set several team records. He led the team back to the playoffs with a 9–7 record. But Washington lost to the Packers in the playoffs. The team fell short of the playoffs

WIDE RECEIVER SANTANA MOSS

ROBERT GRIFFIN III

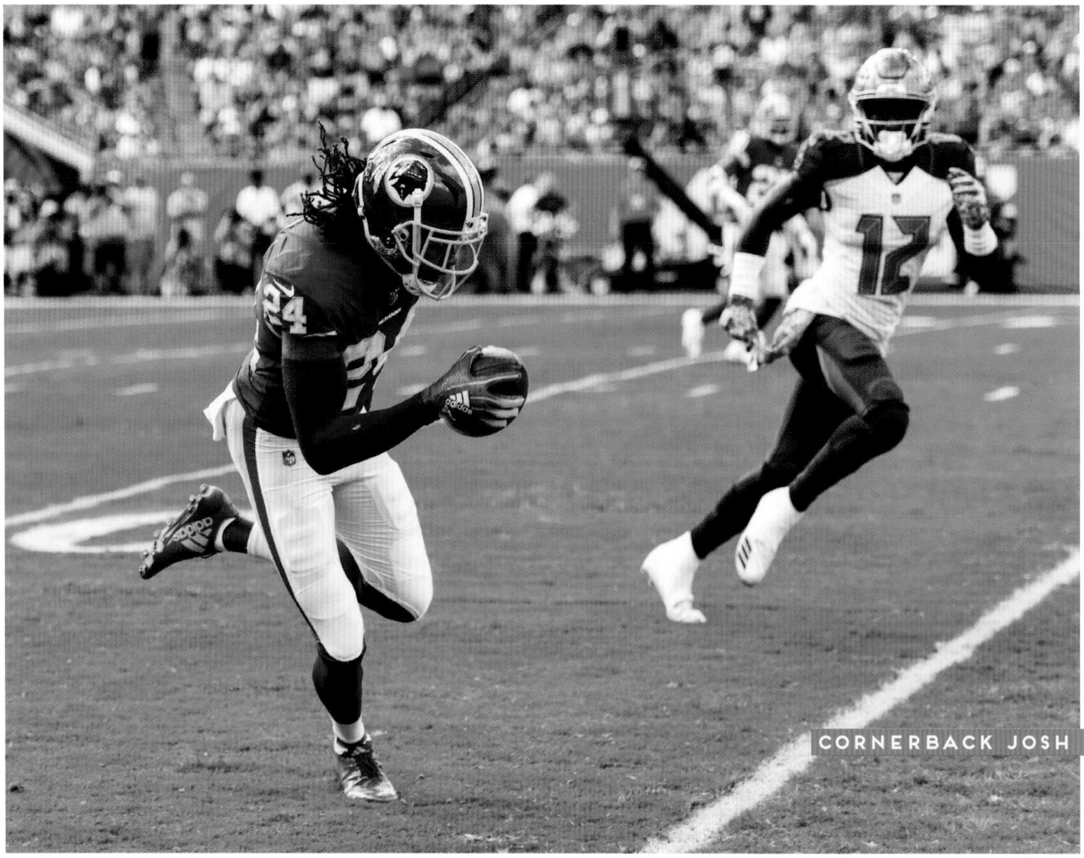

CORNERBACK JOSH NORMAN

in the next two seasons. Then Cousins became a free agent and left the team. Once again, the Redskins had to look for a new quarterback. They added veteran quarterback Alex Smith in 2018. In Week 11, Smith suffered a compound leg fracture. Various backups tried to fill the gap he left, but the team won only one more game. It finished 7–9.

The Redskins have been part of Washington, D.C., history for more than 80 years. During that span, they have won several championships and developed some of the sport's greatest players. They have suffered through losing seasons, too. But fans trust the tradition their team has built. They are confident that Washington will soon be the football capital once again.

TEAM STATS

NFL CHAMPIONSHIPS

1937, 1942, 1982, 1987, 1991

WEBSITES

WASHINGTON REDSKINS

https://www.redskins.com

NFL: WASHINGTON REDSKINS TEAM PAGE

http://www.nfl.com/teams/washingtonredskins/profile?team=WAS

INDEX

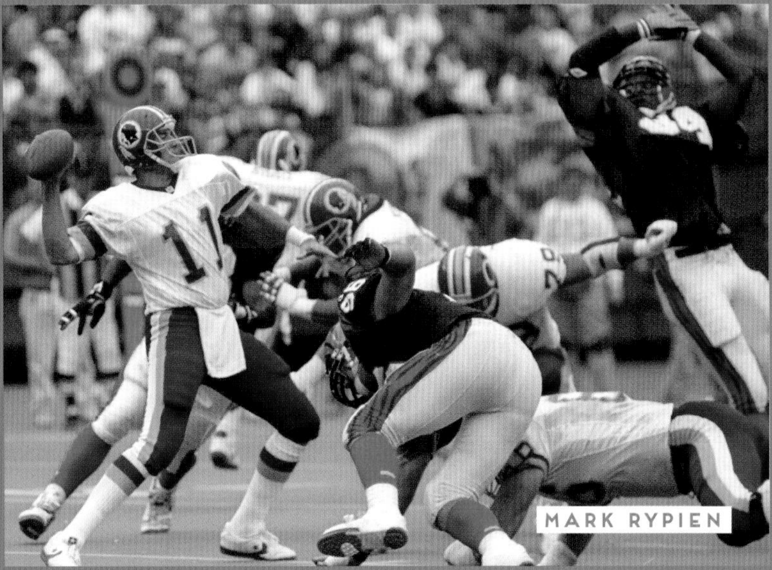

MARK RYPIEN